CW00796418

THE LAST MUSEUM OF LAUGHTER

d/e/o

NEWTON-LE-WILLOWS

Published in the United Kingdom in 2014
by The Knives Forks And Spoons Press,
122 Birley Street,
Newton-le-Willows,
Merseyside,
WA12 9UN.

ISBN 978-1-909443-35-8

Copyright © David E. Oprava, 2014.

The right of David E. Oprava to be identified as the author of this work has been asserted by him in accordance with the Copyrights, Designs and Patents Act of 1988. All rights reserved. No part of this publication may be reproduced, stored in a retrieval system, transmitted in any form or by any means, electronic, photocopying, recording or otherwise, without prior permission of the publisher.

dedication

from
ocean *to sky*

the way
a river
is only a name

for water
never twice
the same

today
you are
the rain

i. the wet song of laughter

ii.   the winter laughter dreamt

iii. **the laughter woke again**

iiii. the quiet laughter stole

iiiii. the dance laughter wore

iiiiii. the home laughter song

...as if laughter were a time machine...

the wet song of laughter

the future's tense

maybe it's only   a calendar
in the outlines of   suckling
silence   before it was broken

we find lost keys   there's a quiet door
or virginities   back when cooking
so long ago left   was an opened tin

within the noise   it hurts to look at
of being in a hurry   like the last time
blurring the lines   you make love
between gash peach   ever
plum & gravity   scrubbing

cleaning   you sit in that square
the kitchen   encircled by greasy
the cooker shifts   dust
on naked floor   you begin to laugh

once again   as if laughter were
exactly as it was   a time machine

the past's imperfect

of all the old things in the drawer
in the house for a new one
that need fixing as he looks at you

there are several saying he'll change
calling a head shakes

with wails broken only
whistles has one shape
wallops one purpose

& so many one name
have been broke he'll find anew
so long with water

it's a sombre moment who's happy
for stalking air to love him

to explain you turn away
that no amount of talking to the sink
is going to replace so tired of tepid
the heating coil glad you've found

there's not a new source
enough change of ocean

the perfect's present

two planks in the floor   used for kindling
have grown apart   you walk over
one bends west   with a blanket
the other north   looking like new love
through a crack   laying it on the boards
lie the remnants of frost   we lie down
cupping the violence   looking at the ceiling
of winter   unraveled

in places no warmth   we can see stars
can go   heaven

I try to fill the chinks   & a future
with scraps of laughter   right
left over from dinner   through
long ago since   the restless

the quiet's express

sometimes	of panic
you wake up	like the green of
realizing	a pond
you're on a train	agog with algae
or a bus	which gives way
or a plane	to willow trees
surrounded by strangers	who have no idea
still sleeping	where they're going
with no ticket	except towards the sky
wondering who	blue
the driver	& a better view
might be	of the park
there's a moment	someday

the ocean's broke

what you felt	was going to plunge
was me	all you loved
losing myself	to the bottom
as if your bags	worst of all
were on a ship	those bags
that set sail	held your
'round midnight	voice
trying to sneak past	the only lighthouse
the harbormaster	in this ocean
as you stood	as it steamed
on the wharf	past the point
knowing it was doomed	you heard beating
feeling	where I was
the Kraken	alive
a Whale	nearly
the Whirlpool	dreaming

the day's pane

in the middle of this	I'm happy
dawn sits	every second
on the sofa	you sleep
like a man-child	plugged into
who won't get a job	the dreaming
with time	blenders
to play	of this kitchen
three card monty	where I've turned
with amo	the colour blue
amas	into something
amat	edible
in ghosted language	that sits
growing the smell	waiting for you
of vanilla	on a dish
beneath	that looks
the vaults	softly
of laughter	like a window

the lime's light

have you noticed daises
the future's started getting their act
growing out back together
between the stumps I swear
where they'll burst through
wood smoke the seams of heartache
likes to laugh there's no need to bother

I've built the years of weather
a porch already on the way
without a house will just have to live

so we can sit with us as neighbours
to sip tea maybe someday
& spit we'll get rocking chairs
watermelon to keep time
seeds with forever's
into the ragtime birthday

the sea's come

not everyone can sleep	on the wagon
on couches	for weeks
as if they were made	knowing
of hay fever	if the sofa
or freight trains	were a boat
while others	it would get caught
call them home	between
like the vagabonds	a look to the sky
we are	from sea
even under	who would open
the roaring	floodgates
of jets taking off	as we cling
we can dream	to cushions
of the rain	crying so hard
away	from laughter
from dry	only some
ground	can fathom

the shadow's elope

the garden's	who live
cool right now	in the arc bush
as if it spent	behind the pear tree
the night	making me recall
growing smooth	antennae
soon to be	on snow plows
smuggled	who live so dark
along with us	north
onto the nearest	talking
shadows	in their whale songs
obscenely tall	we're so close
lavender stalks	to drifting
bent	across the border
by bumblebees	before sun will notice

the tone's akin

it's the sound	calling
when the rain stops	3am
& the bed	hello
is an unfinished ark	at the laundromat
in that hollow	with solace
you wonder if	maybe before light
you're a dream	a clean start
being lost	will somehow
or sown	make the dawn
in a field	honest
of rings	& explain
with keys	what she's done
on the phone	with silence

the alarm's question

it's very possible	shouldn't the day
that this	once it's done
has been	open its fist
my job	to say here
long since	cool air
before	it's your turn
I was ready	but no
to wake each morning	these bricks
at exactly	& these boards
four-thirty	are stubborn
& open the windows	clinging to the heart
of asking	of a sleeping sun
how a house	as if tomorrow
can be lonesome	was a question
forgotten	I am here
by love	to pull up the covers
still holding	to gently
a heat	give you
so wrongly	an answer

the mystery's can

there are some days	reading directions
when yesterday	in the language
finally closes	of the future
the door	unsure
he won't call	would it taste better
any more	tomorrow
or send cards	but with a hint
or chocolates	of reckless
you're left	you get
in the kitchen	the tin opener
with a life	& a spoon
in the cupboard	because
behind the canned goods	time
just waiting	only gives
to be opened	so many presents
so you take it down	when you came
put it on the table	I knew
just to stare	the taste of
at its face	yes

the wet's missing

I'm sorry   as mine broke
about the mess   most likely
in the kitchen   from lack
I think   of sleep

I must   so
have borrowed   if you need me
a little madness   I'll be out
from this heat   in the garden
where   trying to call
everything   the rain
including the wind   & cleaning
has lazy fever   the mess

I was trying   left by
to create   living
a phone   so far
from something   from
savoury   welcome

the bob's dozing

it's like a truck stop   with no
of clouds up there   where
while blue   to go
takes the day off   but toss

which is nice   then
as sky pulls on   roll
my tender   & bob
grey   on the whispering
t-shirt   bed-
in the quiet   clothes
of a day   you've drifted
that doesn't have   off
to stir   while I've been
yet lying in bed   smoothing

making small   the whole
paper boats   idea
from   in
silly stories   the first place

the meadow's tune

captain	I am
of the great	in the architrave
meadow ferry	of listening
free for folds	to a glass
in time	of wine
light	in the distance
carries us	a rooster
through blue grass	confused
to the jazz	by
of a tree	existence
playing green	feels
as the sun moves	the presence
'round the madmen	of a chopping
called flowers	block
who battle	a road
with bees	a sunset

the hell's dammed

curse	the desert
the lack of clouds	believing
& everything	words
said aloud	are sung
the air's	instead
become	of being
a hermit	gut-shot
& that being said	whose pain
no creature	is too prolonged
would ever listen	instead
to a voice	of death
who has	who dreams
no song	of better things
the echoes of wrong	of
ringing the walls	no one
once upon a time	come swiftly
I'm sure I safely swore	I'll birth
I'd never be a sponge	my own
or lick the keyless ring	soft
yet here I am	ocean

the forever's almost

the giant steps	& then some
of water	as my ripples
freckled by raindrops	fly
by the old mill	to their death
whose stone	over & over
is gone	again
& boards	as they say
are loam	of graveyards
my companions	folks are
as I stand	dying
in the store	to get in there
watching	so I watch
the sale	the brook
of fish	inviting
flown in	my soles
on astral planes	like eggs
sea-	you cooked
bound	that morning
all we have	we were
is wet	easily over
forever	almost

the boom's starboard

how to love three sheets in a bed
the perfectly of flowers
broken who could
in a field possibly sink
of swoon this ship
& a barn of sun
beside I say

begging to gulp standing on
a few drinks the lightning
with rods of this day
goats where we are

dancing hopelessly
to garlic singing explosive

the smile's pipe

how many	I know
are built	how rotten
on broken	the roots were
yet grow	yet we
as if the air	shake hands
was made of legs	half-hugs
& their arms	like matching birdsongs
held on to clouds	somewhere
to become	in the sunshine
these stunning	that comes
willows	from eyes
spied	watering down
with affection	the shadows

the nature's strange

you meet nature   feral
everyday   knowing
never giving   there's no way
it a name   to be anything different

except for tremendous   as the grass
tremble   gets up for work

as the tree   sun sings
looks back   for her supper
to say   accept

you were the same   you & I
as children   were never
I remember   danger

the finale's rain

I'm afraid	that says
the grass is broken	party
the dust is bitten	as tears drop
it's funny to think	the porch gives way
that somewhere	from garden to beach
someone	to ocean
is crying	where funk
for a million reasons	& bass
I like to imagine	just married
in this heat	the wind
a lover's just come	in all her jealousy
to the back door	sucks the ocean
who hasn't been seen	clean
in decades	while sky
brought	having watched
with them	everything
a breeze	can't help
wrapped carefully	but cry
in polka dot paper	at weddings

the sun's socket

I've hidden   **the bulbs**
a bottle   **out of daylight**
of wine   **before the sun**
in the laughter   **realizes**

let's get naked   **no one's**
in a meadow   **really**
screw   **paying**

the organ's flower

have you heard   laughing
this rain   senseless because
as if the air   the rain
won't stop crying   has nothing

like all sad movies   to say
at some point   but sorry

you have to laugh   we
let loose   always
the wallop   end
that becomes   up
contagious   naked

as a chorus begins   an organ
of people   with so many
in motel lives   petals

the love's hurt

I dreamt of   love hurts
old beach houses   but unrequited
& people   is worse
whose lives   as the screen door
were standing   slammed
on cliffs   I swore

waiting for the wind   tattoo
in a kitchen   THAT
speaking of indecision   on your forehead
I ran through   with no idea
looking for beer   if dreams
yelling   can really listen

the air's space

they say   this is all I ask
the crack   leave your
of icebergs   scorching husband
can be heard   have a fling with wet
from outer space   & put this
& volcanoes   in your pocket
with their screaming   as you go
can make the sky   it's the smallest box
unhinge   of laughter

I'm spending   I'd like it delivered
all my money on   today
plainly   I'm afraid
simple   it's all I've got
air   until they find a way
throwing   to fit the voice of oceans
her a party   within
with a pension plan   the cloud song

the everything's left

nothing | seated
will be all right | next to desire
the child | will always be sin
will still be frightened | & nothing
by the under-toad | will be
as the sea | perfect
could care less | if it were
if we skinny-dip | we'd miss
& naked | the bungee cord
will never be | of breathing
in fashion | we'd miss
unless we grow fur | the human
for skin | friction

each day will begin | & we
when the clock | would sleep
says so | forever
& time | with nothing
will always | left to worship
be slow | & nothing
as we wait for | left
love dinner the bus | to
an elevator | ruin

the static's charm

that was a late night   in the static
a loose whisper   eight times
under the covers   the clock rang
holding a tin can   nine times
& string   it rained
stretching   ten times
'cross oceans   a new day

damn I'm tired   born
but smiling   while we lay
knowing we were   in each other's folds
overheard by whales   hands on our hearts

& cockles   watching the dark
who sang   do somersaults

the pavement's lot

on the last day	the pavement's
of school	far
parents	less
wave off	even
their kids	surely
as if	the waves
it's the vestal voyage	are calmer
of an ark	as each of them
& the children	head off
are so light	to build
they almost float	their own rafts from
aboard	silence

so free	& secret plans
of baggage	to sail

while adults	way beyond
linger	the familiar
in the playground	to a laughter
counting	our luggage
the bus tickets	won't
already squandered	let us
& surely	imagine

...as if we'd never **discovered** *crying...*

the winter laughter dreamt

the salt's ice

once lived in a sea	it was broken
with chinked walls	by the weight
so wind	of its beauty
could live there	at minus forty
too	for a month

it was so cold	by zero
we rained in a bucket	we got naked
that froze each night	exactly

solid	how
thick as salt ice	neon
in my beard	feels
a sky so blue	to nightfall

the ghost's glacier

this quiet's	trying to smooth
never	the waves
complete	from sound
there's always	even ice
something	cracking on the porch
forming	is distant
trickling	like the ghost
grinding	of a glacier forming
even in the calm	in bed
light	the static
a hum	is jammed
coming from	like a traffic
over there	of thunder
behind the sublime	a desert
under the coarse	as if we'd never
carousing	discovered crying

the hat's you

I need a hat	down in the darkness
to hold	your breasts calm
in my thoughts	my grizzled
to temper	songs
the frost	trying to blanket
this moon	the lonesome
you cradle	holes in clothing
gets frozen	doing nothing
when the wind	for the bones
wakes up	just send me
after the bed's	a hat of you
gone to bed	like a corset
where my moods	to hold
grind	my darkest mountains

the light's old

each morning	shaped like stars
I go outside	having almost
before dawn	fallen off
looking for	nothing seems
the north	too far
star	surely we've sung
through a pane	before
the tree's	this hoar
lights limber	swaggers
so cold	as if he knows
with silence	the answer

the plum's brandy

those smells   of country ghosts
of love   your nice
on the stove   round laughter
fish cabbage   fits warm
& potato   in my hand

there's rime   as you cook
on the cobbles   heaven

somewhere   I sleep
back east   on the floor
in blood   of old souls
salt is singing   who've come
freshwater songs   to listen

the call's lost

it's like trying	whispering
to find keys	bawling
you had only	where this should be
yesterday	under the sofa
or love	in the shed
when it's been so long	maybe the store
just an imprint	has some left
on a pillow	or no
the smell in a teardrop	maybe we've pinned
this is winter	too much
when it's raining	on the present
when you know	pick up the phone
if it were just	& hope
an inch colder	wherever they are
there'd be snow	they're drunk
if clouds could just	on that spark
combust	you've mislaid
there'd be stars	perhaps
& halos	in last year's pockets

the eve's because

you'll have to listen warmly   from here
this year   sailing with sheen

laughter has decided   gathering quick
to amble   on love's gravity
taking the long way   you must look out
home   softly
to the moment when   from your window
was it snowing   this morning
were there evergreens   if there's sun
know   or snow
someone   a sparkle
somewhere   even mist
in the world   will do

has always been yours   that's me

perhaps   landed on your door-
you've never known   step
that's how gifts unfold   & we are
so I've put my laugh   you may recall

in the air   a present
like an aeroplane   from past
that grows   to wonder

the blue's welcome

must have laid	the dog
that beauty	& tattered gloves
round here	of restless
somewhere	to herd miles
damned winter	of broken air
blooms	hungry for
like summer rotted	bedroom smells

so much	barely
the eye caterwauls	smacked
at its tantrum	into air

yet	blue
by the slim gun	fallen
of noon	on this snoring plane
there's only sheets	across
of sheer	pillows

or drab	your eyes
so I've	tornado
unwound	welcome

the draught's call

it's hard to tell	sniffing our letters
if the lights	for perfume
are dying	or cash
to rush back in	I use
or whether	the hard
they're waiting	parts
for one last kip	of my body
in the	to sculpt draughts
cool	into curves
before sleep	shaped like you
seems to me	letting curtains
that dawn bolts	do exactly
with theft	what
in its bag	they're
like a mailman	paid for

the blind's lighthouse

down	like all things
on the beach	it will
telephones	get lighter
are ringing	as the storm clouds
in the new year	of weddings
planting	buried
stars	within the ocean
that will mark	let go
the death	their
of gravity	baffled
that's passed	sirens

the what's wicked

what if the sun	without you
went away	but see
for a few days	the sun's
off to the beach	thinking
or maybe mountains	the same
for the first few hours	damned
you might think	things
this is ok	as he's
like frost	away
before the bite	visiting in-laws
after that	stuck on the moon
you wonder	in traffic
is it ever	took a wrong turn
coming back	but he'll be back
& that's when the panic	because he wants to
comes home	because he has to
that place	without you
in the sky	there's no need
you took for granted	for me
you tear	to
thinking	keep
I can't live	erupting

the breakfast's sky

went out	no winter thoughts
to see the moon's	till I land
bare feet	on pilgrim rock
on the forest floor	then walk
wondering	a little softer
if I keep stalking	I should be there
could I gather	by morning
enough mass	will
to build a boat	you
round my cross	make
the sea's	my favorite
not far	the murmur
if I'm lucky	of thunder
they'll be	calming

the bomb's softy

the red   I will
of a mother   exploding
sleepless   with the gentleness
as she listens   of flowers
to the crack   across her neck

of her universe   her breast
who will care   & eyelids

for her   I'm oceans
in need of tender   learning to swallow

the dream's levy

sitting by the window   under the roof
made of natural sugar   yet to be built

like a pane of milk   all that stands
I'm trying to make art   is the window
from matchstick men   through which
on the pine table   we guess at
we don't yet own   the future

but someday might   drunk
next to the bed   on each other's
that hasn't broken   hopeful

the time's served

dreams   without
are prisons   whom

dyslexic   life would be
heavens   a sentence

the warm's bed

turn down   **like**
the sound   **laughter's love**

explode   **was**
to warmth   **homeless**

the wood's mirror

the mirror   polished
is lousy company   & waiting
it's like a calendar   by the window
with broken clockwork   cum daisies
I farm dishes   before daybreak
to take my mind   barefoot
off the fool   counting
hunger   holes
in the sky   in the floor

a book of still-lives   once limbs
penned in glitter   sawn off
I flicker   now bored

kicking   I talk
the patois   to the wood
of chain & stone   mooning

I should   so soon
walk   the worry lines
like light   uprooted

the choice's deal

it's your feet in a bed
as they play that matches
on the porch the walls
tapping the windows
into the roots all of them made
that run from old
under the floor doors
taking their highway borrowed
across fields from barns
into the woods schools
where you lie naked wedding halls

in the ferns each one had
I follow their moment

the footsteps open
of every year or close
since that first & we chose
snow gods know

taking off my clothes we're chosen

the leap's faith

as if the month   found the present
had dressed itself   you left
backwards   while I was showering

I did   a sundial
the same   just waiting
with my shirt   for batteries
jacket   which I put
pants   on the dashboard
all facing front   like a savior
while my feet   jumping in
& face   I turned the engine

cruised the past   combustion
within my heartbeats   forever started

the blue's green

so many times	hell
woke up	only
on the wrong side	the phone line
of a bottle	living
broken	like a nun
by the fieldstones	saving me from
unearthed	green
by a plow	electric
that's my inheritance	I drop a dime
how it pulls me	watch it
through	groping
things buried	at the speed of static
by misplaced laughter	over the blue
in the morning	to the bed
the yard's	I should be in
wrecked	hello
my hand's missing	it's
a gut full	me
of mountains	endless

the smart's woman

I don't know   where I belong
where   there are stars
anything is   storming
the breath   beneath the sea
to clean my glasses   who say
the cloth   get off here
to wash   this is your planet
my nethers   unhinged

I can't find   let the smart
the words   woman
that fit my palm print   untie
unlike your breasts   your heartstrings

who sleep   she's clever
pale   her boom
unbroken   her bye bye

help me find   she doesn't care
the echoes   about
to locate   your blindness

the time's now

a meteor	comets
blew up over	misgivings
somewhere	& I don't know why
it broke	I'm here
with its mother ship	the sky giving
kicking	no answers
satellites	laughing
in the socket	at the next rock
while below	to roll
in a snow bank	across this winter
I sat lingering	with tumbling clouds
next to a steeple	of exhaustion
a clapboard	imploding
contraption	in my bedroom
for praying	where I want
to the monster	to get busy
who made	in case
love	it's the big one

the day's too

today	is not a knife
is the hardest day	not a vein
that's ever limped	it's a knot
past me	& the beginning
into the morning	of an alchemy
I take the broken	that will someday
from my sleep	turn years
place it on the floor	who
naked	lived like
like breathing	motel rooms
like beating	into blissful
is not an end	innumerate
today	oceans

the page's blank

this dawn	sea
becomes a quiet love	as pies bake
like circles	poems play
left by	cowboys
the explosions	behind the sofa
of raindrops	our tables
that make up	are doors
gods	our windows
words	milk
& the one foot	while logs hold us
that comes	in a bed
after	we intend
another	to break
all the way	well beyond
to the illiterate	the infinite

the art's sure

there's art   this is it
in the wood   the last stand
of walls   from the lilies

nail holes   you're calling
where buckets hung   with a voice like roses

or fruit   who am I
dying   to hold out so long
in winter clutches   with nothing

between the chinks   his limp
are dust motes   like missives

light on horseback   farewell
laying siege   hunger

I tap the teacup   I'm off
calling shadows   to pluck
to mass   the gilded

the lock's electric

all this exists while we're
quietly apart
in its own time instead
each affair of snoring
of thought aching
action arcing
spark like downed wires

with a slow clock dancing
wandering waiting
after bedtime for spring
in parking lots you're
on dead phones pacing

trying to book as I'm
passage begging
to a socket for the tumblers
a shock to click
the heart like revolvers

to standstill for lips
then start to sunrise
to alive open

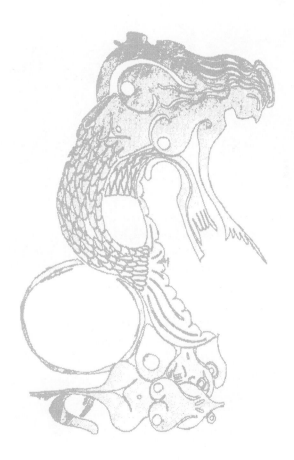

…for lips to **sunrise** *open…*

the laughter woke again

the little's prayer

opening   by a waterfall
the kitchen window having had words
a bull of hot air   with the sky
ran   reminding us
from the house   all the sea
to the garden   ever needs is
where it looked   blue
for the swansong   lips
that was high   her laughter
in the heat   & the cool
all day   morning

yesterday   trumpets

meanwhile   like love
smooth snuck in   whose had
taking my hand   a sip of
& holding it   good
like the clouds   & now
I prayed for   sings
sang   come swallow

the light's direction

I think you must have   the wrong direction
my ticket   you see
as I sit   I want to go
on the bed   backwards
connected to the air   to the place
by a ceiling fan   where it's barely dawn
& open windows   so I can deliver

as if light   these urgent blue
were a train   eyes

I wait   so she'll remember
on the platform   she's no need
looking down   for make-
the barrel   believe
of sunshine   beauty

that seems to be   today's
reeling   infectious

the third's thought

tonight	forget
it's still someone's	worry
birthday	to be tugged
although they're asleep	by a moon
& the world	which is always full
has come between them	having second thoughts
it's comforting	about its weight
that strangers	we sit
will look at dates	so close to each other
& wonder where	chatting with quiet
all the beginnings are	believing
tottering	time has
like drunks	shattered

the voice's hips

sleeping in the garden that held onto heat
I could almost hear like hips
the waterfall of stars in a boat rocking
who had nothing to say & I couldn't bring
except roll on myself
roll to suffer

to the edge of like nails
the dew song for these
who came walls

with a splash not while
of need to be the voice of wind
skinny-dipping was
in air dancing

the god's leg

the three-legged dog	to look forward
of morning	through
walked past	my book
as if the past	of lost songs
had a leash	there's one
wandering away	that doesn't
to summer	belong
as I planned	just bellows
autumn	written by clouds
weddings	I'm awake
& deaths	& grateful
building a day	for the tug
from hours	of blue
of sky	on my shadow

the picture's taken

breaking into   wildflowers
the last museum   we've found
of laughter   the last
a waterfall   civil war veteran
a camera   in a pasture
a car   smoking
in raining traffic   his beard
all passed   fighting the saw grass
at speed   too happy
by natives   with imagination
intent on linear   to ever ponder
time travel   his trailer

not me   his teeth
interested only   in tomorrow

in you   we are fugitives
so smooth   from gravity
your summer storms   & robbers
so loud   on the lam
on washboard gravel   from the last
so stung by   museum of laughter

the rip's bellow

reading the sky   I read a cloud
first thing in the morning   of love-mad
is like a newspaper   artwork
written by roses   that makes me smile

who've stayed up all night   up the rips
painting the walls   of my tides
of space   to bellow

with brushes   blue
made of jet planes   laughter
& contrails   heard
they call daughters   in the vaults

now   of sleepless
& then   shadows

the song's whale

may your day   **drifting out to sea**
be a storm of daises   **where colours**
as so much depends   **blend**
on shading   **with whale songs**

how the bend   **born**
in a river   **to be eyes**
catches some light   **who**
then sheds the rest   **launch**
at sunset   **the bombers**
where half of us sleep   **of morning**

secure   **may your day**
in our shadows   **be halos of iris**

the flower's sun

what the rain holds   with nights
she no longer has   deflowered

pockets for   I'm happy
those stories   to be a ground
never told   for all

I won't wear a coat   her broken lightning
or an umbrella   collecting
instead listen   blue sparks
while getting drenched   & giving back

the same way   the firmament
a sun gets naked   almost mended

the pearl's sworn

a kid   stuck in the craw
in the rain   of something
swore she grew   perfect
a pearl   as she laughed
as I tried to explain   unswayed

it took years   I understand
of crying   this woman

under   her age
water   who turned
& that   pain
it all began   into
with a grain of sand   a virgin

the gentle's history

I should have   & I missed a chance
dipped   to be part
my toes   of a gentle history
in the water   blaming morning
just to get   for me
the imprint   not having dreams
of pebbles   or getting
on my soles   tattooed

next time   on a midnight
they'll be   when nothing else
different   mattered

as floods come & go   but how
whole trees will appear   glad
on the falls   I am
where none felt like   you're
growing before   infinite

the flood's witness

I echo	rocks witnessing
& see	how you've come
your thunder	to a stone
knows where	smiling
to go	at life's geology
down the dirt road	you know
across a bridge	as you tiptoe
rebuilt	the stream
after flood	so cold
frost	I imagine
wind	how gorgeous
so purple	we shatter

the seed's blank

this old house   in hopes
has buckets   of growing roses
of keys belonging   or daises
to dead doors & windows   & sadly
long since   not even a charity
married   will take them
or buried   so they're hung

& there's nothing   from hooks
to be done   seldom looked at
with these jigsaws   or dreamed of

their meaning   unlocking ourselves
gone missing   for the ones
you can't plant them   we need

the book's pocket

the last	I
two matches	knew
left in the box	if I fiddled
were spent	hard enough
bought the farm	with friction
automatons	I could burn
with so much potential	Rome again
just missing	& my pocket
their heads	has become a home
like balloons	for the grins
run out	of lost
of sky	ignition

the moet's potel

I dreamt of the motel   for flowers
          again   who've taken up
         a place   jousting below the tidal
      where words   wave
       can spend   without walls
      the summer   just a roller-coaster
        & change   for whale watching
     their spelling   playing lawn darts

         by the sea   rock-
in small wooden cabins   a-
    built in the 50's   billy

      a motor court   this will come true
    without a king   your invite's
         a meadow   in the tempest

91

the now's here

the here & now	has married
is wonderful	the ocean
as if you're	a breeze
in the other room	walks up
preparing supper	looking
& someone	as good as
has stolen	heaven
the TV	dressed for dinner
along with the walls	& our eyes
of this house	have just won
the sun's	the prize for
a nice	dancing
allusion	blue
& the garden	confessions

the minute's feet

it was dancing	nonchalantly
in the kitchens	into pockets
of boats	& shoes
& farmyards	like notes
where I learned	from the resistance
how to fly	who would not bend
electric	to the clock
sweat & air	exploding
cut into pieces	hours
like minutes	into seconds
small enough	where sound
to eat	weighs more
or thief	than meaning

the eye's ears

you take my glasses   I can replace
off down the lane   my lenses
with the washboard ruts   with rivers
& try to rub dirt   that see you
from the frames   in a valley
where a new house   naked with green
is going up   rolling down to the sea

at the curve   to listen to things
past the lake   only eyes
as my fingers   can hear

dip through   only gravity
water panes   can explain

the ache's head

it's the headache   left open
that grew   where you dream
in the opening pages   high on the wall
of your skin   with winds
when something broke   so strong
& all that's needed   no handholds
is someone   just the grease
who knows   of tragedies

your paleness   I see
to scale   what's needed
with glue   before us
plasters   there was nothing

& kindness   so dream
through   I'll put
this window   my wings on

the gold's fool

I made the mistake   **I may be eclipse**
of reading history   **not epiphany**

of seeing love   **whose shadow**
before I existed   **is fire**

its cages   **the same**
still rattling   **as rain**
& wondering   **frost**
what happened   **roots**
to the words   **all willing**
I've heard so often   **to ravage rock**

before they were mine   **I've 'come**
when they sang   **the shape**
in another's octave   **of earthquakes**
sinking   **barking solace**

the fun's self

all of the apologies   that smashed things
I've been saving   happily
are packed away   so I could
except for one   move on
which I've left   as I get in the car
on the table   empty of bags
next to the fruit bowl   tanked to full

so   you sit shotgun
it won't get   touching the spot
lonely   before baldness

when the sun sets   imagine
& shadows take over   how fun
the rest   I'll be
are going in the post   as the package arrives
to the past   twenty years ago
where I used to have   when regret
a hammer   wasn't an option

the story's hand

I love the story	in the heartstrings
of love	down roads
if love	where bones are
were a person	catapults
they'd be someone	leading to fields
you wouldn't	best laid in
want to cross	naked
after a few drinks	tattooed
with a back	to eyes
broken by bombs	like the sky
still ticking	what love looks like
& a tongue	after decades
rough 'round the edges	of being alive
tired of being bitten	is part dog
instead of sleep	part god
nights walking	worth taking
to check on the stars	by the hand
&	because
cooking	the skin of love
for ghosts	is blindness

the winning's smile

this morning I woke with nice
to the most incredible curves
sadness that normally would
as if it were have made me smile
a prize winning sadness instead
with a crisp I felt like I'd won
blue ribbon pinned first prize
to my chest & they'd left a note

as I walked down saying
the 7am road so
to the corner shop you win
for anything essential in a ceremony

the air was fine completely
like sand & utterly
like an hourglass abandoned

the memory's alone

my phone broke   colours
in the crashes   whose names
of a water bomb   I'd forgotten

war   living
in the garden   under the impression
there was a moment   that all
of electric bliss   of you
as if a dictator   only
had been overthrown   existed

'cause death   inside
ain't got no   that little box
dial tone   how glad I am
in this land   memory

I herd   alone
the soft   can make
skins of voices   you
swimming   gorgeous

the year's ago

at this point   of red & pink
we're using rose bushes   white
like a wireless   with less make-up
nudging sex   than was needed
along roots   before
under the Enola Gay eyes   because

of birds   as voices come clear
who float   there's only one way
seamless   to say beauty

between ocean   I learned
& sky   years ago
while we're decoding   to never dissect
the subtleties   a flower

the affair's state

writing from the land	**up the jet stream**
of not so great	**until they erupt**
I've gone	**a Krakatoa of love**
underground	**we'll proclaim**
to make bombs	**the colour**
of jasmine	**tempest**
rose	**as president**
& honeysuckle	**in a state**
to be lovingly sown	**for the sky**
into birds	**&**
who burst	**oceans**

the dream's fever

the fever dreams   too tired
drove off for a while   to get up

their tail lights   & go to bed
looked nice   instead we put heads
like fireflies   to breasts
in the waggle   & listened
dancing   to the wisdom
wine   of one footstep

while we enjoyed   then another
the quiet   & so on
of dead   till they returned

stars   cooled by dawn's
like rocking chairs   rose engines

the laugh's sleep

& just like that   I literally laughed
the fever is gone   while I dreamt
stolen by someone's smile   as if fevers were sitcoms
perhaps thousands   happy days
of miles away   red licorice
I need to say   a village green
thank you   now all safely
to a sleeping head   tucked
playing a naive melody   in bed

like a broken record   while I begin
for which I have duct tape   to crank up
& a jar   a rose bush
of laughing I saved   telegraph

from the pillow   the only thing
where it spilled   that works

in my sleep   it seems

the door's ocean

before you pack   a child's ride of gears
the bags   outside the stop & go

you have to build   instead
a boat   use the fast lane
finger in the air   of electricity
checking dampness   gravity
will this idea float   the kinetic force of
as we zero   one door closing

the odometer   to push this dream
check   that looks
the roses   so good in blue

slap the flanks of morning   across an ocean
& forget   where the sky is waiting
the sun   with eyes
is coin operated   saying

& goes   they're tears of joy
so slow   honest

*...where the **touch** of wind wears voices...*

the quiet laughter
stole

the wind's call

when they lay	the lick of cannons
the first cable	as you battle
under the sea	behind
a sky	blinds
was still	those eyes
impossible	imagine
like children	we're electric
dreaming	with sparks
only as far	rocking
as their arms	current
out-	like the ocean
stretched	taking you
would let them	to blue
buying	where the touch
laudanum	of wind
over the counter	wears voices
in praise of	a cure
everlasting numbness	for all things
I hear	thunder

the ocean's grog

if you wake   like air
to a bag   itself
of thunderbolts   sat at our feet
at your door   clapping madly
with a note   to feats of daring
that says   in fact

here   I recall you leaping
have fun   from the sun
don't hesitate   to dine on our moon
thinking this could be   in an ocean of gods
dangerous   we were

where do you suppose   till getting
those lines   dressed in silence
on your palms   as if our voices
originate   were stowaways

back in the days   not today
before we had   wake up
knees   naked
to kneel   & run
there were names for us   I'm counting

the hang's on

nothing gives birth	having a blast
thinking	call you
I'm going to do this	on the mobile
imperfectly	hey
not thunder	wish you were here
the sky	what
or supernovae	can't hear me
while gravity	it's loud
gets to work	yes
punches in	what
starts the machinery	don't talk while driving
we're drawn	& somewhere
to the pipeline	out there
by hands	in the miles & miles
hungover	of timelines
happy	fate
or blind	drops some light
86 thousand	caught
400	just before
second	the fall
chances	'cause this floor
per day	we're pretty sure
I'm visiting	is made
the explosion	of nothing

the yawn's long

how is sleep	**with explosions**
anything	**then swept**
but keys	**from the paper-thin**
to the gates	**sheets of friction**
of strange	**2am**
& full	**awake**
of dreams	**time**
we ferry	**seams**
like a bag	**backwards**
of bombs	**like the world**
with voices	**got dressed**
blunted or blown	**drunken**
small words	**we stalk to work**
in a rumpus	**naked**
I can't recall	**they stare**
what you said	**laughing**
just the lips	**deaf**
as if	**to**
you were painted	**loveless**

the clock's crone

there's a missing　　as I sat
chalked up to　　in a prison
daylight　　of travel

there's a boogie　　sometime's
once done　　our pockets
in abandon　　empty
never to be　　of the wish
encored　　to change

if I had　　till we see
a power　　the wakes
it'd be　　in stone
to seduce　　our bodies
clocks　　claim

I knew this　　slow
from the instant　　dancing
I stepped on a school bus　　space
how all I'd ever learn　　in air
would be hair-do's　　we breathe
faces & frowns　　for granted

the quiet's song

they've uncovered   for the ears
the pitch   of love
of space   to find them

it's middle C   I walk through
jangling   with a tuning fork
like a ukulele   on my way
out of tune   to the diner
forever arcing   kissing
to an audience   each one
packed   smiling
with particles   the songs

out of reach   of horns
from solar wind   holes
like a bus stop   & numbness

in the rain   we get notes
with everyone   in rolls
humming   because
softly   it's a long way
to themselves   from here
waiting   to silence

the where's roam

it's just less | in need of new shoes
than a mile | with the most
each way | magnificent necklace
twice | of keys
that's three & a half | look at this one
miles a day | it shook
how far | a blue Monday
could I go | what a place that was
if I didn't brake | & this one
at the school gates | a Friday
but rolled on | I'll never regret
like a clock | & so on
taking its time | till the road calls
in a week | wondering if
the ocean | I'll be home
a mountain | for supper

the sky | kablooming
with a knife | with the hours
in my teeth | left to unlock
oyster beds & mermaids | if only
imagine me | to bare
dancing on your doorstep | my soles
wet | to the pavement

115

the roar's atone

there's no rite   to entice
on how   the otherwise
to love   careless air
the difficult   I'd like to believe
when they're dead   that tune
only a legend   will be hummed
that lives   by children
in freeze frames   who're blind
of remember   to truth
when   a roaring wallow

after that   let them
it's conjecture   believe
& the vanilla paper   in heroes
of history   while I take
does what it will   my honest

I'd like to say   a shot glass
there's a song   now
written down   cracked
for every day   on
we do something   gravestones

the egg's home

the label	out back
on the box	through a card-
says un-	board flap
break-	holding my sky
able	gently
as if egging	to become
baggage handlers on	an ocean
to do	you're welcome
their damnedest	to sit quietly
like lightning	with a drink
rolling up	smoke
its sleeves	& fire
getting pumped	far away
for the doozy	from clocks
not me	mistaken
I ducked	for airports

the flicker's score

the nightly	on offer
picture show	snow
always leaves	leaves
the last scene	cars
imprinted	furrows
on our bedclothes	fanning out
as we walk	into fields
through the door	where time
into daylight	thinks

as if sleep	we're maybe farmers
were a matinee	of lonesome

our pockets full	it took lifetimes
of crickets	to make
bullfrogs	a cast
& open windows	of a million moments

the shadow	this skin
song	the dog-eared script
of a road	a star
calling	the crop-duster
with a million	our hearts
kinds	endless
of soul	projectors

the bolt's shorn

when the truck broke   daily
for the last time   remembering
on a dirt road   the good times
that never had   in the front seat
any intention   how the hum-
of being ruly   torn bearings

the river   could bring us
next door   alive
liked the arc   in rear-view
of laughter   mirrors

in composting colours   thinking
going   we needed
from   a bomb
grey   on wheels
to brown   to get us
to forgotten   from here

as if it were an autumn   these borrowed
mortgaged   graveyards

the light's worn

in case you're wondering while leaves
I'll be packing light play sayonara
there seems to be on cellos of storm
enough to go round wind begins
the photons with hello
in my bag & ends
won't be missed with panting
as I take it with me my feet
down the streets are painting
a hobo a path
solo no one's meant
sung by soles to follow

so good just know
at echoes if you're hungry
we throw I'm passing
leather with time
at roads to share
to applaud your eyes
the rendition will sing
of space the answer

waiting mind
for boot- I call you
falls someone

the ark's warm

the place	died
where people live	doctors
when they're not	dead space
in our dreams	how quickly
must be	they cloud
curiously calm	away
like a static	you whisper
lake	it's ok
so voiceless	but a me
cold	from years
they never	ago
age	is alive
until night decides	in someone's
it's time	mind
as if names	& I wonder
like natures	if I'm living
could change	a motel
I'd call you	life
awake	you open
to be told	your sleep
of skiffs	to me
& sky	like an ark
leviathans	made of heartbeats

the missing's borne

picking up   to brake
where I left off   I hoist
as if right on   what's wrong
was spilled   enjoying
on your doorstep   its weight
while I went   the way
off seeking   a silver dollar
meaning   collects gravity

as if sleep   I write
wasn't madness   on my hand

as if dreams   don't gamble
weren't expensive   & start walking

penniless   lighter
with nothing   for the darkness

the arc's tow

in the library us two
on the bottom shelf who've only just learned
of the kids' box in three thousand
is a book years
that explains that a look
an ark a smile
animals a laugh
rain can be heaven
in 3D let's go
pop-up find a wood
fashion an island
for anyone someplace sound
who wants to understand barring plugs

what happens where the only
when God electricity
hates humans comes in arcs

here lightning
hold my hand & sparks
the flood of news as your feet
blog & ego in socks
is the second slide under
time round my blankets

the story's own

in a time   just be
without much space   where the ground floor
you don't tend   has no literary
to find   aspirations
people living   & breathing is easy
in a single story   because the windows
instead   open their hearts
they're stacked   without hearing

sometimes as many   traffic
as a hundred   dramas
atop the other   or lovers leaping

intersecting   to fall
in elevators   past winter
the sparks   & spring
of plot lines   my smile
seeded   on a hillside
by fate   so sky
if possible   can come
I'd like to be   save me

the horn's blow

reaching back   to something
from deliverance   matters
the buses & streetlights   as I jangle my keys
rock   waiting for traffic
their angry   to swoon
oblivious   the day
to the quiets   to burn
intent on   & time
glazing their eyes   to never
with blinds   return
of blue   in my pocket's
sun   a picture
arcs bowling   drawn on this palm
from the sky   remember the place

you can almost hear   a waterfall
the gears   that belongs to you
of drawbridges   I held that gasp
above the cells   enough within

so busy themselves   now it's skin
holding on   an ocean

the where's torn

there must be	arms
galactic storms	reaching up
that happen	& out
at sea	to explain
& no one sees them	it was only
except for the ocean	a squall
& sky	who's now
scared	moved on
to talk	like a hobo
the next day	wrapped
in case	in the sound
their bed	of all
is made	that's ever wished
with sheets of rain	for a home
instead of waves	to be
leviathans'	bound to

the storm's elope

as if that moon　　at the door
were an ashen　　it's hard
war-　　for light
lord　　to leave
having chased　　home
lesser suns　　anymore
from the sky　　in this garden
leaving only　　I take off
the ones　　my hope
with something　　we
to say　　decide

constellations　　to elope
once known　　with the blessing
can never be erased　　of naked
& the symmetry　　no longer
of lines　　dreaming
like faces　　but
come to court　　doing

what should we do　　what's always
with these wishes　　been written
hijacking space　　just happy
till they wash up　　stars
like storms　　have listened

the know's go

let's not talk about death	like leaves
yet	their encores
instead	those acorns
bedtime	need rest
stories	so we sit
you might tell	breathy
trees	beneath
while they get	trying to siphon
in their pajamas	the orgastic
as if they were kids	from the moment
whose only wish	waiting for a song
is to prolong	of footfalls
the inevitable	yet even they
they invent	are swallowed
plays	by broken
& games	the day
these spectacles	grows daily
to upend	with a promise
the quiet	that springs like a child
of goodnight	I'll wake you
in the end	lightly
their costumes	before the ending

...words are ships for the **passage** *of heartbeats...*

the dance laughter wore

the virgin's reel

as the captain	echoing
comes over	the rustle of sheets
to tell you	on this bed
the ship	where sleep's
will sing	a call
you're still	from virgin
the sky	timbre
I'm	a place
an ocean	where all
that folds	has changed
when it rains	as we pay
words	for the passage
are ships	of heartbeats
who trawl	I fiddle
amongst us	for pennies
what glorious	salt
battles at sea	wind
we sometimes	within
witness	the whistling

the sweet's toll

most beautiful orphan	this baby
today	who has
woke us up	no idea what's going
in our hangover hearts	to happen
banging on the pots	come midnight
& pans	makes me want to buy it
of light	candy
in the kitchen	before
while we're	the matinee
still mourning	supernova
the	all the
dreams	while
born	I know
yesterday	I knew her mother

the lip's pawn

if only   damage
words could   a different
be eaten   laughter
& the clock   a forever
only   fruit
borrowed time   grew
we could return   on trees
to where time sits   as we go
unsold   picking
handing over   the blinding
our ticket   ripest

with a smile   like light
of hands   devoured

reaching out   to be
to last week's   forgotten

the light's home

the tense slice of pear
made by the lawnmower

with its haircut
has answers

points
to the same conclusion
as every eye
in the universe

no number
letter
or sound
can express

as I write a letter
to grammar
asking
to do away
with question
marks
full stops

I would take
the billboards down
streetlights
satellites
'cause nothing
needs lightning
when hope's

& the smell
of grass

pain
is simple

the now's unsound

gentle	this calm
as if talking	reaching
to now	a finger
rounding the corner	within
where	to find a penny
a phone box stands	I pocket
its own peculiar	hoping no one
museum	saw
papered	shocked
with dance	by the sudden
I listen	ring
to the flood	hello
of light	yes
becoming clouds	you knew
no one has	that somehow
known	matters

the marble's bone

some might think   we're sinkable
we're made   yet
of parts   I protest

a fiery heart   perception
cool intellect   & wonder
a dash   if we imagine
of diesel   we're singular
thunder   forged
as we fall apart   from something
each one replaced   simpler
as the mile-o-meter   we won't need
ticks over   a compass

cat eyes   & time
in the rear-view mirror   becomes
force us   an artist
to reassess   who carves
our condition   humble

don't head   ships
straight for that iceberg   of marble

the tide's arrive

what	there's
clouds	naked

may	blue
come	abandon

the gator's stone

I would love   the monkey
to be   across
philosophical   the river

I'd zen   oh nature
the hell   you have so many tricks
out of everything   in store

with pebble towers   karma
to be built   you're gonna have
on every waterfall   to take
in the universe   a rain check

yet   with raging
I'm a chainsaw   to do

like the parable   & peace
where the alligator   makes
almost gets   no promises

the gods' alone

if	of the impossible
every day	as if possible could
had blackboard walls	ever love us back
we'd be kids again	how delicious
with crushes	& painful
no human	that plum
could ever survive	was
making us	how jaded
aliens	we've become
strange	now we have
in our skin	hammers
as if chalk	with engines
were the bones	& a wall
of being young	is just a milestone
drawing hearts	with rose-tinted goggles
with wings	I'm ready
& arrows	for this brand
round names	of rapture

the needle's moan

if the band plays	the table
long enough	turning
there's a dance	to go under
for every bed	the needle
we've ever called	I undress
home	the record store
hanging on notes	& feel
aroused by	so many lives
the trumpet	second hand
bass	running fingers
saxophone	'cross groove
songs played	to revive
in black & white	the heartbeats
as if the crackle	they spun
of hiss	softly
was part of a score	so as
we're vinyl	not
with sleeves of paper	to disturb
taken off	the neighbours

the dancer's load

you were right	awoken
I was worn down	on a pirate ship
by the nighttime mood	of dreams
of the day	playing poker
so I let myself go	with words
to be navigated	a flush
by nothing	of heart ache
dropping needs	I learned
like breadcrumbs	how to sea
a trail	making the sky
I'd never follow	a beacon
again	trading my hands
letting them find	for seasons
new homes	walking the beach
as if they were	with a ballast
playing cards	of dance
in the universal	& a highway
deck	dressed
we share	like the ocean

the stone's unload

while you're here in a café
let's compare with canals
ourselves all around
to shipwrights as boats
who speak whizz by
in oceans on bikes
& inland in every shape
rivers & sound

whose words lavender
are made rosebush
by hammers cloud

& cannot do rocking
in one day reminding
what it takes there's never
to understand truly
roads solid ground
clocks just the way
weather we comet

sand sky in hand
we're sunning to land-
down fall

the air's goad

whoever invented   in the park
        nerves   of circumstance
      had some   I'd like to send you
     maybe then   my stalking
    they sparked   dreams
          booze   slowly
       or sleep   learning
       anything   the balance
  to make us numb   between

         as a kid   desire
I never liked see-saws   patience
   never trusted them   air & ground

     as I watched   pointing
   too many mates   gravity
        jump off   all in the same
      at the last   direction
        second   attraction
         crash   like a hand
      conundrum   like a song
       swearing   all there
    I'd never build   to teach
    a playground   nerves
    yet here we are   a lesson in laughter

the stop's rhythm

you'd think	to dartboard
the city could never	stop
be lonely	I feel so
with all	irreparably human
its human gears	more akin
in fleshy	to the urban
syncopation	alien
spilling	of a river
enough friction	beating
to fill a stadium	the band
of lovelorn	for an ocean
except	while the sky
I see nature	tunes
gallons of fish	blue
& pigeons	ignoring
wheeling	the
fortunes	rhythm

the never's twice

down the creek road	while the radio's
where ruts	playing
have voices	a song
of their own	sung by the sky
the air's	that says
dug a home	the river's
in dirt	just
that likes	another name
just about	for water
everything	never twice
including thoughts	the same
on a getaway	like you
sixty miles per hour	like today
past timothy grass	as it trails off
chewing itself	always
in the sunshine	trying

the blue's grown

the air's	cider
starting to crisp	who sneaks off
like an apple	in a jug
getting ready	under the bed
to leave	to grow
the airplane	something stronger
of leaves	than frost
to do	we're in the post
the Newtonian	called sleep
belly	waiting to be opened
flop	seeds
to become	feel them
a poster child	eager
for blue	to burn through
ribbon pies	the dreams
rosy cheeks	of calendars

the cover's under

the cold shower   to the floor
needs no towel   miles down
only a t-shirt   flying
in front   in flocks
of the fan   of dreams
whose hum   & all
does little   the maybes
to soothe   of dark lips
the thunder   in the shadows

building steam   of daybreak
above the rumble   waiting
of a heartache   for the laughter

with hands   of a single
smoothing   shaft
the sheets   of lightning

of rain   climbing
as they tumble   under
from the bed   the covers

the lightning's lost

sometimes rain always born
runs the way with the seed
of light for oceans
painting sown
gravity in our soles
on a windscreen without feet

dust or heart
has all day to get there
to gather only this engine
its thoughts & ashtrays

these streaks full of wild
of lightning lost temptation
looking for clouds to ram
who let them these gates
free fall on the toll road

we feel from here
like orphans to heaven

the dancer's canon

when the show's over   where quiet songs
the curtain of rain   lie on their sides
comes down   like seasons
as dusk   toppled over
brooms the stage   we wander
of any heat   touching each one
leftover   with no bullets

you & I   left to hollow
hold onto our seats   you pocket
while the masses   a pinch of this
imagine lovers   a pull of that

saying   mementos
let's peek   for perfection

one more time   now it's cool enough
behind   to call the kitchen
the foggy shower   our dance hall

the bed's gold

it seems	clean as new snow
I've never	ready for praise
had the patience	which is a term
for real hot water	for the already missing
perhaps	I'd miss being half-
it's kept me	washed
just ahead	hungry
of the trouble	from days
one lukewarm bath	of smoke
after another	sunk like bottles
keeping my eyes	in the backyard
on the prize	where I used to dig
a name given	sure I'd find
to someone	the lost ark
not home	of your smooth
& what if it came	amused by my sweat
that elusive now	repeating
I'd have to shower	your heart
to scrub off the years	as I bathe
as I power down	a reward
in a halfhearted dance	is the name
so I could stand	I've given bed

...the songs of sky **unleashing** *her ocean...*

*the home laughter
sang*

the dip's skinny

I wish	too many times
I'd dreamt	trapped
of your garden	with no means
clogs	to change
grounding	the spelling
the weed	of dreams
whacker	till
on a pillar	I gladly
of mermaid curves	switched
followed by	channels
summer showers	where
explosive	you were
instead	still
I swam	awake
on a page	fishing
of words	deep
ones	into
voiceless	my morning

157

the road's apart

packing	hard
for a small trip	by the onslaught
a trip so small	of heat
you could almost	this summer
pack it in	has brought
with the books	but the weather
bedding	isn't at fault
& underwear	will never be tried
I found a magazine	locked up
you bought	as I pocket a small
with pictures of homes	ceramic heart
we almost	glazed in blue
could have built	& white like the sky
as if	a key
we were gods	I so often forget
with magic hearts	to hold
to make beaches	let grow
skies	as the hips
& rocks	of ocean
I almost cried	road
my mind	& wave
candy	undress themselves
brittle	like laughter

the lip's leviathan

& this   one wetter
is how   than the other
I come   I'm not fully awake
with surf   just drifting
at my feet   somewhere between
wondering if   high tide
beach creatures   & roadside diners
measure their lives   part man

in six hour days   half leviathan
half dozen nights   with nothing to do

while clouds   but give in
linger in layers   to the lips
like levels of dreams   of undertow

the light's deep

it's easy   where lives happen
to forget   at the sound of light
rain   beating
if we live   our universes
underwater   while below
playing with   in a place like dreaming
gigantic   the dark explains

whose laughter   rain
is carried   to the deep
piggy-back   who tries to
by the fathoms   imagine

like long distance   the songs
phone lines   of sky
at home with crackle   unleashing
& hiss   her
here on the surface   ocean

the snap's boom

in the barking	gears
clockwork	& fulcrums
of morning	to spin
the sun & clouds	& send you
are musicians	a ticker-tape solution
in an audition	while I take one more
for some	snap
dream-fed emotion	of daylight breaking
who said	her one-hit-wonder
nothing	firestorm
will ever change	hoping
because you're not	wherever I am
here	you feel
you're waiting	the force
for the cogs	in chorus

the hope's plunder

maybe it's	near noon
a press gang	this cloud
of wind	loses dreams
up in the shanties	like a homecoming
vividly	where seas are
reeling	leaden
while our captain	hear ringing
the pole star	from this crew
bellows	of stars
from below	us pirates
keep spinning	come moon
lost heavens	come rude
keep wheeling	& death
'round the capes	of grey
of longing	to hope
sweet fear	for plunder
god laughing	from lightning

the talk's small

it was a small talk   before
over breakfast   she ran off
about if fish liked   to sing
or disliked   a song
water   I hoped
as the child   to bottle

who had to count   & share with you
on fingers   in some dry
like toes   future

said no   as if that rain
I don't love   could never
or hate   be sung
the air   again

the angle's rose

after the roses	each one
have gone	taking turns
to wherever	an oar
flowers go	in the ocean
& the phone lines	the other
lose weight	skywards
through a fast	from a distance
of fists	they punch
what once felt	in quiet circles
like a battleship	lifted
of laughter	on the
becomes	birdsong
a row boat	the only way
drifting across	I know
time zones	how to grow
so slow	from this
that silence	angle
explodes	even shadows
to the same size	are
as words	ennobled

the bomb's begin

it's ok	to step out
to wake up	the door
winded	looking
to little frogs of fear	for buses
scattered	meteors
as if	knowing it's
they'd once	a bullet
been something	with the guts
larger	to go miles
like a	in the palm
whale	of a fist
now pieces	if you wished
of blue	you could burst
you could put	this damnation
in your pocket	a kiss
bite-sized	begins
adventures	eruptions

the sound's novel

there are rites   to make songs
in drops   that sound
of water   like a novel
who collect   being
their tribes   written
on the cliffs   by rain
of branches   frost

& the commute   I once thought
you   only
dreamt of   the sea
where we walk   could save me
along walls   perhaps
made from rocks   I was
grown in woods   wrong

become fields   it's the ritual
swapping crops   of being
of light   rhythm

from eyes   letting
to close   go
us two   of all
kicking leaves   the tinder

the river's body

it's the day   towards midnight
you put to bed   bells
with all its noise   call time
like animals   over
crowded   a body
'round the pillow   of water
to whisper   never
while we go   crossed twice
to the other room   as eyes
to uncork   which held
the air   red laughter
that's been building   are still
a clinic   & the bed
to fix the waves   is a ship
in sound   peddling

flowing   new boxes
out the window   of rivers

as the clock works   just waiting
like a waterfall   to be
wishing   upended

the how's soon

soon	was a tidal
no one	printing press
will remember	each morning
what it was like	reliefs
to smack a TV	rolled off
to get rid	the breakers
of static	with visions
clinging	like birthmarks
to the belief	I wore
that violence	till the next circus
will somehow	yet here
smooth the airwaves	I wish
& I woke	I could
today	play with
in the aftermath	the rabbit-eared
of bad reception	antennae of time
being	while you're off air
inland	after the anthem
has stolen	static stared
the clarity	at long enough
of my dreams	becomes
at the beach	a new
the ocean	religion

the sky's neon

if only we had pictures   yet today
of voices   I'm wearing
some so new   a black
their laughter   seamless shirt
rocks off the paper   without a collar
in horny blues   in contrast
& crimson   to the rough
while others   of my cheeks
are faded   with white
in a sepia   in my hair

whose smells   what voice
have songs   do you hear
of their own   when I plug in
& I want   my eyes
your sound   as they blink
in my pocket   with electric
the breast one   sky
where I've kept   neon

lilacs   sung
roses   to the chord
honeysuckle   come hither

the song's silence

how to get a tan   in the silence
from a star   unbroken
light years away   by sirens
stand naked   or cliffs
in the yard   just waves from space
at 2am   saying
surrounded   be loved

by darkness   on a ship
which   with four dimensions
if you look down   you're plucked
could easily   from the present
suck you in   given a blanket
to everything   on the deck
that lives   & head off
in the bags of years   in a new
you've brought   direction

anger   watching your bags
jealousy   be eaten
pettiness   by rosebuds
if you're lucky   back
there's a song   in the garden

the told's truth

to tell	how happy I am
the truth	to know
it's a beautiful day	the name
both	of laughter's
out & in	lover

the break's fast

with the sun	arcing
sleeping in	pretty sure
a little longer	the molecules
each day	that make up
the clouds	locks
are getting	are
creative	sadness
with musical scores	picking
they tried to arrange	up
before	speed
they thought	like marbles
I'd notice	let drop
not helped	on this ocean floor
by the gulls	that's always
hoping to harp	wobbled
as you bend	hope in the clock
in the shower	brings
thinking	cloud songs
velocity	for our
gravity	breakfast

the will's matter

the air wore a different / speechless
coat / because my words
last night / were resting
as it rode the train from / in a bed
waterfalls / I'd found
out west / restless
where someone built / only so much
pebble towers / boom for me
to defend against / & heaven
leaves who've been / I don't mind
put on trial / by morning
& found guilty / they're architects
by a child who knows / off to build
more about things unseen / things
than us ever / with matter

as if the garden was / given love
a papier mâché platform / like water

a cooler breeze / between us
left the carriage laughing / likely to lure
with song I stood / the distance

the word's other

when lightning strikes	words
is it over pay	& dreams
or perhaps tired	stranded
of carrying	wearing a t-shirt
a sea	in the rain
of oohs aahs	that says
& arcing	open
along its back	heart
as it stands	hyperbole
in the picket line	not sure
blocking the way	what to do with
to air	these replicas
bus wind trains	lifted
stuck in the city	from
after a day	the gift shop
of sightseeing	in the last
the architecture	museum
of people's	of laughter

the comet's soft

a folded paper sky softness
came in the mail & news
today that goes unsaid

you wrapped it you're still undressed
in blue just the cotton
which was thoughtful that hides
more a present your naked
to the ocean as if it were made
who found a reason from clouds
to get my imagination
out of bed has stronger powers
& sit to unwrap
in the garden the package

counting the pears of sun
already falling you sent
like comets tied

we talked about with the faintest air
time of wetness

the rain's bowed

somewhere   a tape measure
in the house   of salt
a clock   distance
is counting down water
to a place   storms
it doesn't know   amazed
as I search   how such
to ask   a small tool
if it could also on a spring
be counting up   & a spool
of course   can fathom
the clock   expression
doesn't care   rapport
either way   sensation

like hair   I hear
growing   the ticking
time   translation

the rain   now
is back again   to throw
to explain   the bow lines
there can never   & walk
be enough   through
as I pull out   the telephone

the laughter's bust

there's barefoot to laughing paintings
on the pebbles whose expressions
of a waterfall we've gladly stolen
& there are stockings & I forgot to tell you
on the bedroom floor in the boot
there are stories of the car
behind each wall there's a blanket
in the courtyard some stars

where flowers & a bomb
have taken time I know you
into can handle
their own hands softly

as we walk BOOM
through the pitch- is another
pine halls word for
drinking toasts beauty

the bomb's forever

to what end	that never need explode
do we owe	like a clock
this pleasure	always stuck on
who's built four walls	naked
housing us both	a dream
through black	maybe
& shimmer	a ticket
I think	to get us past
it's perfect	the present
nothing more	someday
than a cabin	this place will belong
on rich land	to children
between the legs	a museum
of stony walls	to the booming
& a pond	song
whose spring	of laughter
is fed	& oceans
by winter	forever
bombs	skywards